MIND BODY BEDTIME

Peaceful Games to Make Kids Sleepy

By Susanne Benton

For my daughter Lucy

So many bedtimes. So much good.

TABLE OF CONTENTS

FOREWORD

Gentle bedtime routines can be hard to find. Days are filled
with ups and downs, physically, mentally, and emotionally.
Navigating these days can be challenging. By evening,
bodies and minds can be exhausted but still restless. This
book is designed to help little people (and big people)
settle into peaceful sleep, and show parents and kids how
to use relaxation techniques to connect to each other at
bedtime. With practice, Mind Body Bedtime helps you
and your children transition to sleep with grace and joy.

"HOW DOES THIS WORK?"

By noticing surroundings, sensing the body, and creating
positive imagery, your kids will build mind-body awareness
skills. They'll develop resources to support their own sense of
self, feel safe in the world, and connect to others with love.

In just a few minutes per day, these mind-body bedtime
games will help you and your child to create moments of
magic, love, and connection that bring your minds and
bodies into a peaceful state. With practice, these moments
can grow into longer moments and can become a quiet
trusted place in which to rest at the end of the day.

These mind-body practices also train your brain and
body to relax, rest, and turn your attention inward, away
from the hustle of the day. Through repetition, they also
teach the brain and body to use self-soothing skills on a

daily basis. You and your child will feel lower stress, less anxiety, and an increased sense of peace and confidence during ALL parts of the day - not just bedtime.

Each page of this book has a different game that connects parent to child, or child to body using imagination and body awareness tools. Each game uses simple mindfulness skills such as:

- positive thought
- awareness of breath
- sensing your own body
- offering love and kindness

You'll notice that as you try out these mind-body games, you create magic! You come into the present moment and shape it peacefully and lovingly. Not only are you actively fueling and restoring the brain and body, but you are also gifting your child with valuable resources for navigating life's everyday challenges.

If you use these games on a regular basis, both you and your child will benefit from increased:

- Body awareness
- Gratitude and positive thinking
- Connection to others and to nature
- Unconditional love
- Peaceful breath
- Mindfulness

WAYS TO USE THIS BOOK:

These games are designed to be played during your bedtime routine. Everyone's family has different things they do as part of bedtime, and that's great. I suggest adding mind-body time as a way to invite kids to slow down and connect-perhaps as the very last part of bedtime. For example, after teeth are brushed, and baths are taken, use these games to move kids toward getting comfortable in their beds.

Each of the games has a few simple instructions. Below the instructions you'll find an explanation of which mindfulness skills are being used and how they benefit the body brain and spirit.

There is no need to do the games in the order in which they are listed in the book.

When you're ready, simply open the book to any page and try the game you find there.

Or, you can read the book from beginning to end, trying the games as you go. After you've tried them all, pick out and repeat your favorite game until you are ready for a new one.

I hope that this book brings a bit of magic to your bedtime routine. Be creative and make these games your own. Change the stories or the visualizations to match your family's interests. Have fun. Be peaceful. Connect. Sleep well!

FLOATING
FEATHER

Look up high and imagine that you can see a magic feather floating high above you.

Imagine you can see that it is _____(color) and it looks soft and fluffy. As you watch, it floats gently and ever so quietly down toward you. As you breathe gently in and gently out, you watch its peaceful, slow journey and imagine that it will land softly on your body. It might land on your belly, your chest, or your forehead. Imagine that it will land wherever would feel most comfortable. As you breathe in and out, the feather floats around above you and gets closer and closer to your body. As soon as it lands on you, you feel calm, cozy, and sleepy. This feather now sits softly on your body. After this feather falls, look up and imagine another feather slowing taking the same journey down, down, down, to you. Each feather that lands on you makes you feel cozier and sleepier.

HOW THIS HELPS:

While imagining a beautiful feather, your mind focuses on creating something of beauty. It trains your brain to notice beauty more often in the world. Watching a feather slowly float down also brings your mind into the present moment and encourages peace. Breathing calmly and steadily helps you to feel relaxed and still.

SEND A STAR

Pretend that you are looking up at a sky full of stars. Imagine that they are all twinkling, but one particular star seems to be twinkling brighter than all of the rest. You notice that its light is pulsing to a beat that matches your exact heartbeat! Put your hand on your heart and feel your heartbeat. Now watch as your star slowly drops out of the sky and comes and lands right in front of you. Imagine that you can fill up this star with all the love in your heart. Imagine that you can send your star off to someone who needs a little extra love. Maybe you send it to a special person who lives far away, or to all the animals that live around the globe, or to everyone on the planet! After the star is filled with love, picture it flying around the world and delivering love to whoever needs it. As you fall asleep, pretend that you can see your love filling up your special people or animals. Imagine that they start to sparkle a little as they are filled up with your love.

HOW THIS HELPS:

When you focus on love, you aren't distracted by negative thoughts from your day or worries about the future. The body has a chance to calm and restore in the moments that you are focusing on stars and love. The act of giving unconditional love to the world or to another makes your child feel important and connected. It teaches that love can be felt by others as it is sent out. It supports the idea that a child's love is strong enough to make an impact around the world.

TUCK ME IN

Think of your favorite animal. Is it big or small? Does it move fast or slow? Is it furry or smooth? Is it a pet or an animal who lives in the wild? Now imagine that you are this animal and you are very sleepy. As this animal, what do you need to be tucked in for a cozy night's sleep? A soft place to lie down? A bedtime snack? A song or a hug? Let your parent tuck you in as if you were this animal. If you have the time, trade places and take turns tucking each other in.

HOW THIS HELPS:

As you imagine yourself in the body of an animal, and decide what you need in order to feel most comfortable, your awareness is brought to the body and to the moment. Imagining comfort brings a real sense of comfort and relaxation to the body, allowing it to begin its journey to rest and sleep. "Tucking in" is an act of love. Offering this love to another creates a sense of connection. Practicing compassion and care for the natural world, as well as other beings, makes kids feel like they can make a difference through comforting and helps them feel connected to the larger world.

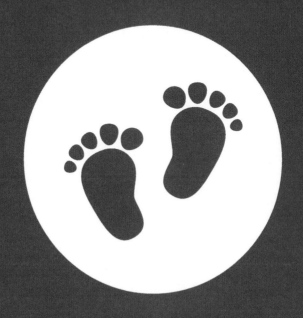

RUB RUB

A soothing touch can help relax the whole body. However, you don't need to be a massage therapist to do it at bedtime. Hands and feet are an easy place to start. In fact, rubbing points on the hands and feet can have relaxing effects on the entire body. Below are some instructions for how to begin a simple and short massage. As you go through each step make sure your touch is providing comfort. If at any time, your child does not like a certain pressure or placement, adjust your movements so they feel comfortable. Show your child how they can do these movements on themselves to help calm their bodies.

For hands: Hold a hand in yours and rub gentle circles on the palm with your fingers. Next, gently squeeze each finger and move it in a small circle.

For feet, if they're not too ticklish: Place one hand on the top of the foot and gently rub the bottom with your fingers or palm. Softly squeeze each toe and move it around in a small circle. Using your fingers or thumbs, rub the top of the foot from the toes to the ankles.

HOW THIS HELPS:

Awareness of your body supports healthy growth. Spending time with gentle touch and massage creates good feeling bodies. Massage is a loving activity which makes kids feel safe and connected. Massage also relaxes and supports tired muscles and tissues, and can soothe away stressful thoughts.

PRETTY PALMS

Put the palms of your hands together in front of you or put the palms of your hands together with a loved one. Feel the warmth in your palms and begin to imagine a beautiful color forming between them. Picture that beautiful color flowing out of your hands and into your body. If you are touching palms with a loved one, see the color go into their body too, filling you both with a beautiful, calming color. Feel your body relax as the beautiful color spreads to every part of your body.

HOW THIS HELPS:

Bringing your attention to your hands brings your mind into the present moment. Feeling your palms pressing into each other, or together with someone else creates awareness of the body, the self, or a profound connection with another. Using color to visualize this is a powerful way for kids to conceptualize the sensation they feel.

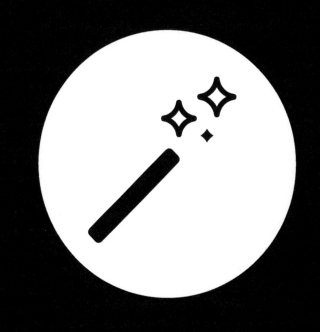

WISHING WAND

Reach under your pillow and pull out an imaginary magic wand. Describe how your wand looks. Pretend that this magic wand is for granting wishes. Think about if there was a wish that came true for you today. If not, what were a few happy moments from your day? Think about a few wishes that you would like to grant for the people you love. What happy moments would you like to grant for someone else? Pretend to grant those wishes before tucking your wand safely back under your pillow for the night.

HOW THIS HELPS:

Sifting through your day and being appreciative of happy moments is a gratitude practice that supports positivity. Granting the wishes of another person expresses love, compassion and connection. Taking time to create a series of positive thoughts increases feelings of well-being, peacefulness and safety, three important elements which support falling asleep.

BED BUBBLE

Shape your hands into a circle. Gently blow through them as if you slowly blowing up a bubble around you. Take a deep breath in and send another breath through your hands. Continue slowly breathing in and blowing out until the bubble is as big as you want it to be. Maybe it's big enough to surround your family or even your house. Perhaps your bubble is small and close, just big enough for you. Pretend that the inside of the bubble is a cozy, peaceful space, filled with your favorite color or favorite music. Imagine that your favorite color or sound is making you feel calm and sleepy. Curl up and fall asleep inside the bubble if you want to or let the bubble float slowly away from you as you drift off to sleep in your bed.

HOW THIS HELPS:

Using imagination to create a safe space is a powerful practice of self-soothing for a child. In order to relax the mind, restore the body and eventually fall into peaceful sleep, a child must feel safe. Having the choice to include your family, friends and community in this safe space teaches personal power and connection to the larger world. Focused breathing brings awareness to the moment and relaxation to the body.

DREAM
TRAIN

Imagine that your bed is a plane train or another vehicle. Climb in and get comfortable. What do you hear? What do you see? Is your seat soft and comfy? What things around you make your body feel comfortable and safe? Put your "sleep belt" on and imagine that you are chugging, flying or driving off to dreamland.

HOW THIS HELPS:

Noticing comfort levels and working to make yourself comfortable provides great body awareness. Becoming comfortable in the moment helps to reduce stress. Being able to make yourself comfortable in any given moment is an empowering tool for kids.

THANKFUL
PAJAMAS

What are your sleeping clothes?
What do your pajamas look like?

Tonight, as you put on your sleeping clothes, think of things that make you happy or make you smile. For each piece of clothing that you take off or put on, share something that you are thankful for.

HOW THIS HELPS:

This small practice of gratitude can help shift anyone into a peaceful state. It can be silly and short, or full of appreciation. Bringing attention to positive aspects of the day can change the body's chemistry to support peaceful sleep and happy dreams.

WINDOW
WHISPERS

Look out your bedroom window (or an imaginary window) and notice what you see. Is it light or dark? Do you see any people or animals or plants? Can you see the sun or stars or moon? What else do you see? Whisper goodnight to the sky, the grass, the moon, the trees, the cars, or the houses. Send a goodnight wish to everything you see and imagine that everything sends you a goodnight wish right back.

HOW THIS HELPS:

With your eyes, you are connecting to the world around you. Imagining that you can communicate with the air, trees, moon and sky offers a connection to the natural world and helps to create a sense of belonging. Sending well wishes and love out your window to the world, even a small part of the world, promotes a sense of positivity about the world that can help to soothe anxiety.

YOU'VE DONE IT!

Congratulations. You are on your way to creating happy memories and connections with your child at bedtime. You've just played an important role in showing your child that they can find peaceful, safe, and connected moments that support their health and happiness. You've just spent time unplugged and focused on each other, restoring balance for you and your child in this busy, fast-paced, distracting world. As you gain practice with Mind Body Bedtime, you will be able to more easily navigate challenges of bedtime (and beyond) with grace and confidence.

ABOUT THE AUTHOR

Hi! I'm Susanne Benton, author, nationally certified massage therapist, former daycare director, and founder of Mind Body Bedtime. I spend my days helping massage clients, having fun with my family, walking my beagles, and finding quiet moments for myself and those around me. It's my mission to celebrate the magic that comes with spending time with kids. I love to write and teach about using that magic for healing and happiness. To learn more about Mind Body Bedtime techniques, books and classes, or to contact me, visit mindbodybedtime.com.

As a small business owner, I am blessed to have found wonderful support to bring my creations to life. It's an honor to work with other small business owners and entrepreneurs. Together, we lift the level of beauty and love in the world, one project at a time. For this book, I collaborated with these two skilled business women, who are also mothers and artists:

Brittany Kalscheur created the image for each Peaceful Game.

Kari Stetson designed the layout and cover art for this book.

Thank you both.
Much Love,
Susanne

Made in the USA
Monee, IL
29 December 2021

87293104R00021